Through A Dark Glass

Maggie Ridge

BookLeaf Publishing

India | USA | UK

Made with ❤ on the BookLeaf Publishing Platform
www.bookleafpub.in
www.bookleafpub.com

Dedication

For my Family

And in honor of Tal Mack, who encouraged me through Word Books, made space for me to gaze out paned windows between chapters of Emily of New Moon, and reminded me that it's never too late to start running.

Preface

I began writing in the heat of summer, surrounded by sirens and suffocation. Against this backdrop of fear, I read *Man's Search for Meaning* by Viktor Frankl and began to listen to my own voice as a way of surviving. This collection of writing is some of what I heard.

Acknowledgements

Mummy, Karen, Sky, Abby, Ed, Lee, Ian, William Keator, and David Peck - For listening to my voice and encouraging me to use it.

2020

That year we just waited for it to end
Some of us partied
Some of us died
Some of us donned face masks
Some of us went to school - Like normal
Some of us worked harder than ever
Without ever going to work

Some of us cried
- All of us cried
Few of us laughed
Most of us watched tv
Many of us slept
And many didn't
Couldn't

Some of us saved lives
While the rest sat and watched
Or made it worse
Or stayed inside
And prayed

As sirens on and on droned past the windows
Women had babies

And children played
The sun kept shining and the sky was a kaleidoscope
of pastels and neon orange
It rained a lot
And the air was warmer

We cooked more
We zoomed more
Businesses changed
And many also died
We clung to little things

It reminded us of our frailty
And the necessity of gratitude
And the mercurial nature of humanity
- a willingness
Or unwillingness
To adapt

That year was almost over
And people kept dying
While the rest kept figuring out
How to live

My Necessary Friends

Lithium, with diligence and patience
and your effective elemental force
You pop in to greet me every day;
A little capsule of protection -
How proud I am you're not a larger dose

I find safety in your daily gifts; reassurance and stability
You keep me firm and you make me fat
I promise not to climb too high or run too far or drink
too much
Lest your delicate effects evaporate
Lest days go past before you fill my blood
Oh little Lithium you save me when I stray

Your friend Lamictal - not so nice
Large and round with powdery residue and devious
intent
I've been told I need you
But I hate you - Disintegrating in my mouth
Clogging up my throat with nausea and resentment

Go away and leave me be!
I don't need you, want you, and there is no pregnancy
So if I choose to give one up, it will be you alone

Clonapin, I love you
Small, round, yellow, pearl of joy;
Peace and happiness and calm
Your tiny, generous gifts
You're worth more than all the rest

You are restricted;
and all the more delicious for it
Once a night, I am allowed
To partake in your soft shroud

Would that there were only you
That you alone would always be enough
Like white wine and sunlight
Or soft evenings under stars

Alas, you never are enough
to save me from the dire straits
Of lost sleep, black holes, confusion
And forgetfulness

When all is lost, I call upon the Dark Lord of them all;
Zyprexa – just as his name suggests - The Beast
Only he can lock me out from my reality
and bring me back again, two days later,
Into semi-normalcy

But why must He exist?
I didn't ask for this.
I wish that He would leave me now
Along with all the pain
He has come to take away

Yet all of them are my defense
Up on the shelf they wait all day
Until "pillitos time" arrives
And I must swallow to survive

Grief 2020

A siren
   and a siren
a siren

   and a sound

One neck knot
   Two neck knots
   One shoulder muscle tensed
Breath catches in throat

One body in the apartment over there
   Slumped against the door, in tears

One body in an oxygen mask flat out
   in the ambulance

One body here on the couch
   stuffing earplugs in to quiet grief

One body here soaking in a football game
   pretending it's normal again

Three bodies in the ambulance
        hoping it won't be another one of those nights
        but knowing it will be

Six parents at home
      knowing their children are exposed nights in and
out
      and hoping they don't return with a noose

Two hundred eighty one thousand bodies
        gone   gone
            Suffocated

Millions of bodies
Trying to celebrate, and live, and smile, without one they
love

No Bars on Bergen Street

The smell of beer in mugs on table tops
is faded

I don't eat there anymore
I just drink wine on the kitchen floor

flatbush x lefferts

a grandmother with her shopping cart

a father with his cigarette
outside the chicken joint

three teenagers
laughing and scoffing down the sidewalk
like they own it

and they don't know yet
about the sky moving behind them
or they're pretending not to

Veil of Time

Turned on by the changing seasons
and cold air from the open window
soft warm cotton flannel shirt, snug

Lying here, blankets on the couch
wriggling toes in soft socks
wrapped in my hoodie

On the other side of a veil of time

I am sixteen again
in warm car rides
through worn down streets of Boston
duplex houses of light blue, light yellow, and grey
graffiti on fences and old bars;
some open, some boarded up

Grey air, cold
Passing by, a stray citizen,
bundled up, lugging bags
or pulling hood over face, huddling,
walking grey sidewalks alone

The quiet rumble of cars

and an imagined promise of what's to come,
something inside perhaps:
a daydream, or a wish

It turns me on, the memories of youth:
the freedom of being taken places
not needing to do anything but stay warm

Foreboding cold transition air
lonely orange leaves clinging to branches
no snow yet, not cold enough to be winter
but just to feel like it might be,
very soon

Dreaming of days I'd be on my own,
parted from the care of adults

Here on the couch now,
toes cozy, resting
muffled whoosh of cars outside -
otherwise quiet
cold air at the window

on the other side of a veil of time

Beach in September

the beach growing up summers
clanging of the metal rivets and hooks on a flagpole
in the breeze on a quiet afternoon or a storm is coming

sound of the waves
weathered cracked paint of the fences and windowsills
and doorways

dune fences, small gaps, skinny slats, broken and bent
over seagrass, gray houses
waiting for occupants to enjoy the view

for a storm or a sail or rain or sun after a storm

sky like an endless changing tapestry of clouds over
shades of blue
quiet summer, end of summer, September afternoon

end of summer is the best time;
no crowds, no noise; just the waves on the shore,
booming of the Atlantic boats waiting in the harbor

except for the clang on the flagpole
the granular sounds of sand against concrete and sandals

tiny yellow, and sometimes purple cupped sea flowers,
edging their way up the picket fences outdoor showers,
not being used

sea sand, gray bird feathers,
our attempts to keep things painted and pinned;
no match for nature
or growing up

Yellow Bomber Jacket

and that's the way she stood there
Just like that
in her yellow linen jacket

I wore it years after that
I loved it and lost it
but never forgot
how she stood with her hands in the pockets

her mouth all scrunched up
her eyes to the sky
"Well, I'm smarter than you"
she was saying inside

Christmas at Gibson Hall

It always is the issue:
how to get the damn tree out the door in January.

One year Daddy sawed off all the branches -
stripped it almost to the top.

She thought it was the funniest thing she'd ever seen
— hated Christmas.

My mother's idea of a great Christmas tree
is a naked trunk
standing like a shamed mannequin
in the massive bay windows of the dining room.

She suggested we use the image as next year's Christmas
card;
as if we ever sent them.

Thanksgiving in Dedham

Again, across the veil of time, with 16 years behind me:

It is a time of smoke from fires just beginning inside and
fires still burning outside;
leaves in woodpiles of yards
of large houses in the suburbs.

My sister and I stayed together in Ellie's attic room
with her RISD paintings, 1980s hair scrunchies and
chucks; feeling traitorous surrounded by the Nobles felt
flag and track team photos left behind.

magazines with ads of Christie Brinkley in her tube
socks and skin tight Calvin's stacked against the wall

posters, left by her older brother,
of Raquel Welch with tanned and oiled skin in a gold
bikini
and Jane Fonda in her lavender leg warmers and leotard
covering the walls alongside John Adams' signature,
etched in the attic beam.

the Atari game we snuck onto Skyler's computer to play,
laughing about made-up words,

playing "trick the parents",
and wondering what it might be like to have Skyler as an
English teacher, or as a mom

A pause
A home that felt more like home
A walk around the neighborhood with the dog du jour
Turkey leftovers and grownups talking downstairs
Nothing to do but read
And daydream
About cross country running
And boys
And days we'd be on our own
Parted from the care of adults

On the other side of a veil of time

Yellow Bomber Jacket ii

I tried

The last time

To capture the youth and breeziness of that yellow linen
bomber jacket

Was she really thinking "Maybe, but I'm smarter than
you" as she scrunched up her face and rolled her eyes to
the sky?

Was I being fair?

Did that jacket mean as much to her as it did to me?

If she knew about the ink stain that bled across the seam
of the cuff, that made me feel less than cool,
or the tear in the elbow where it was worn out – with
love!

If she knew that I discarded it in a bag to Goodwill
she'd have surely thrown a fit.

I tried, Mummy.

I tried to get you to bring us home home that day after
school;
not to spend what felt like hours,
talking shades of white and eggshell gloss at the
hardware store -
to convey our hunger, sweat, fatigue, discomfort

I tried to love that jacket as I have you – precious, free,
defiant, cool, soft, unique, with pockets into which I
might shove my fists.

I tried.

Is it fair to say that you did too?

Memory Sheets

On sunny days in bed
memory comes like sheets overlapping

The sheet of 1995: arrival in New York City
Yellow Rat Bastard and the rock opera *Rent*
the giant Levi's store downtown, giggling with other
girls, trying on daring tube tops, wearing plastic chokers
too young to understand
the shattered glass at Urban: an intentional brand marker
-always wondered.

The sheet I can't recall if it was real or in a movie:
yellow summer fields and a white farmhouse
tall wheat soft through fingers
a rough lichen covered stone wall under palms
climbing astride it under August heat
watching light dance on leaves of a friendly tree across
the road
the smell of dust from truck tires

But maybe it was just pictures of old fashioned pickup
trucks
just the memory of the *Betsy* books that came from the
daydream

inside a 6th grade classroom, looking out the window at
brilliant trees,
winking through ages old glass in a clapboard building.

memory sheets layered;
as if to be touched or plucked up and tasted
like a sweet tasting listerine sheet
or a magical candy from the Wonka factory

Haiku - PSH

A flower is born
inside it blooms, then withers
crushed amongst the weeds

Dark waves take hold
the self is shattered by them
the spirit is lost

An idol is dead
Confronted, the heart bursts forth
forcing a new life

Lilian in Moonlight

No, you said.
So I sit here on the fence,
quarter moon hung high
St-Germain in one back pocket,
phone in the other,
"Revolver" on full blast in my ears

Virginian sweet nights;
filled with crickets by the thousands chirping
me, not in bed

Hard wood against thighs;
not your hand, not your touch
just all the universe
and me

Under the light of a gazillion stars
and the waning moon
I could ask why a million times
but this is all there is

A cool breeze
Sweet grass filled air
My Cape Cod sweatshirt

My fading mind
"Stadium Arcadium"
and the memory of you

Up and Down the Boulevard

3:4 time measure of the guitar solo cowboy
accelerates so quickly

Strangers always quick to sing it drunk
somewhere they must feel the weeping plaintive voice
of those opening lines

Could one dig it so when in despair:?
the emphasis on "get my FILL"?

No one ever listens to the way it really is
because they've heard it so many times
"on and on and on and on"

"the movie" never ebbed soft or sweet

More Than Enough Ways

There are more than enough ways
To fill a day
But in the background of December grey
Is you

Screaming at me
Neon blinding

Legs at 2:47am

All day I thought of you
Now it's 2:47 am and sleep hasn't arrived

Raindrops on the window comfort me
even in my agitated state
(or is it just the wine?)

I pause Taylor Swift to examine my right calf:

The Band-Aid over recent safety pin scratches
(I forgot the antiseptic; it didn't hurt as much as last
time)

Hairs I haven't shaved in a while, lingering around,
waiting

A bruise halfway up
(or is it the blue toothpaste I used to cover the bug bite?)

Hidden in my upper thigh, the scars of the scratches
from last month or so
(that you ignored)

You didn't really ignore them, but they made you mad

And when you saw me you didn't ask after them
(You maybe wanted to forget)

I never told you about the little burn scar
from ten whole years ago
when every day I held a lighter to my hand
to escape the pain of a mean girl clique at work

I should really shave my legs.

My cat is like you; judging from the windowsill:
"What you really need is not to shave those legs, but to
go back to sleep"

I press play again and Taylor nails it (as always):

"We found Wonderland, you and I got lost in it..."

(Taylor Swift, "Wonderland")

Wednesday, 2:56 am

It is at these hours that I contemplate the vast weight of
a black hole as compared to the enormity of my love for
you

and the existence of ancient aliens with my house cat
who reads me like a book and dreams of the moon.

Girl With Figs

Oh how she missed the cafe car
because she closed her eyes
and imagined herself the sort of girl

(young - not 46 years unwise)

who would always carry little cups of applesauce
and a tangerine for a snack;
or figs and a bit of cheese in her pocket.

Then she was so light she floated on the tips of trees.

a rehearsal

My tears are dry because I'm in the shower.

Every heartache of my life

was just a rehearsal for you.

Dishes

Faucet dripping
Weighted blanket
heavy with guilt

I promised and promised
It's all you've ever asked
I can lie here and stew
in my sweaty sheets

The cats can cry
and the teapot shriek
But nothing moves me

And I wish I'd washed dishes for you

9 789369 540723